JAMESTOWN
*H*eritage
READERS

Book AA

Lee Mountain, Ed.D.
University of Houston, Texas

Sharon Crawley, Ed.D.
Florida Atlantic University

Edward Fry, Ph.D.
Professor Emeritus
Rutgers University

Jamestown Publishers
Providence, Rhode Island

Favorite Children's Classics

ILLUSTRATED BY THE BEST ARTISTS
FROM THE PAST AND PRESENT

Jamestown Heritage Readers, Book AA
Catalog No. 950

© 1994 by Jamestown Publishers, Inc.

Cover and text design by Patricia Volpe, based on an original design by Deborah Hulsey Christie
Cover and border illustrations by Pamela R. Levy

Printed in the United States of America

1 2 3 4 5 HA 98 97 96 95 94

ISBN 0-89061-950-6

C·O·N·T·E·N·T·S

ONE
Tales Retold

TWO

Here and There, Then and Now

THREE

The Whole Story

UNIT ONE
*Tales
Retold*

To Market, to Market
from
MOTHER GOOSE

To market, to market,
To buy a fat pig.
Home again, home again,
Jiggety-jig.

Where, Oh Where
Has My Little Dog Gone

from
MOTHER GOOSE

Oh where, oh where
   Has my little dog gone?
Oh where, oh where
   Can he be?

With his ears cut short
   And his tail cut long,
Oh where, oh where
   Can he be?

The Traveling Musicians
by the
BROTHERS GRIMM

A donkey once said,
"I am hungry.
I will go to town
and sing for my supper.
I sing well.
Braaaaaaay!"

He met a dog.

"Come with me," said the donkey.
"We will sing for our supper."

"I sing well," said the dog.
"Bow-wow-wow!"

"Braaaaaaay!" said the donkey.
"We sound fine together."

13

They met a cat.

"Come with us," said the donkey.

"We will sing for our supper."

"I sing well," said the cat.

"Meeeeeeeow!"

"Bow-wow-wow!" said the dog.

"Braaaaaaay!" said the donkey.

"We sound fine together."

They met a cock.

"Come with us," said the donkey.

"We will sing for our supper."

"I sing well," said the cock. "Cock-a-doodle-doo!"

"Meeeeeeeow!" said the cat.

"Bow-wow-wow!" said the dog.

"Braaaaaaay!" said the donkey. "We sound fine together."

Soon they saw a house.

They looked in.

No one was home.

The people who lived there were robbers. But the animals did not know this.

17

They saw food in the house.
And they were very hungry.

They had a fine supper.

Then the donkey said,

"Soon the people will come home.

We can sing for them.

We will sing for our supper."

19

Soon the robbers came back.

"Braaaaaaay!" said the donkey.

"Bow-wow-wow!" said the dog.

"Meeeeeeeow," said the cat.

"Cock-a-doodle-doo!" said the cock.

They thought they sounded fine.

But they did NOT sound fine
to the robbers.
They sounded frightening!
The robbers ran away
and never came back.

So the animals
stayed at the house and
had many fine suppers.

Snail

by

LANGSTON HUGHES

Little snail,
Dreaming you go,
Weather and rose
Is all you know.

Rub-a-dub-dub

from
MOTHER GOOSE

Rub-a-dub-dub,
Three men in a tub,
And who do you think they be?
The butcher, the baker,
The candlestick maker,
Turn 'em out, knaves all three.

The House that Jack Built

from a traditional nursery tale

This is the House
that Jack built.

This is the Malt,
That lay in the House
 that Jack built.

This is the Rat,
That ate the Malt,
That lay in the House
 that Jack built.

29

This is the Cat,
That killed the Rat,
That ate the Malt,
That lay in the House
     that Jack built.

This is the Dog,
That worried the Cat,
That killed the Rat,
That ate the Malt,
That lay in the House
    that Jack built.

This is the Cow with
     the crumpled horn,
That tossed the Dog,
That worried the Cat,
That killed the Rat,
That ate the Malt,
That lay in the House
     that Jack built.

This is the Cock that crowed
in the morn,
That waked the Cow with
the crumpled horn,
That tossed the Dog,
That worried the Cat,
That killed the Rat,
That ate the Malt,
That lay in the House
that Jack built.

This is the Farmer who sowed
    the corn,
That fed the Cock that crowed
    in the morn,
That waked the Cow with
    the crumpled horn,
That tossed the Dog,
That worried the Cat,
That killed the Rat,
That ate the Malt,
That lay in the House
    that Jack built.

Hickory, Dickory, Dock

from
MOTHER GOOSE

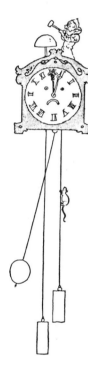

Hickory, dickory, dock,
The mouse ran up the clock,
The clock struck one,
The mouse ran down,
Hickory, dickory, dock.

The Heron and the Fish

from
AESOP'S FABLES

The heron was looking
for her breakfast. She said,
"I want a big fish."

A little fish swam by.
"Too small," said the heron.
Another fish swam by.
"Too small," the heron said again.

No more fish swam by.
So the heron had no breakfast.
She said, "Next time,
I will not be so picky."

UNIT TWO

Here and There,
Then and Now

Androcles and the Lion

a Roman myth

There was once a lion
who had a thorn in his paw.

He roared.

He cried.

He pulled at the thorn.

But he could not get it out.

A boy named Androcles
had run away from
his cruel master.
He came upon the lion.

"I can help you," he said.
"Give me your paw, my friend."
And he pulled out the thorn.

Later, some cruel men
captured the lion.
They captured Androcles too.

One man said,
"The lion is hungry.
He can eat this boy."

So they put Androcles
in with the lion.

The lion roared.
Then he looked at Androcles.
And then he gave the boy
his paw.

The men cried, "What is this?"
Androcles said,
"Once I helped this lion.
So he will not eat me now.
We are friends."

Friends

an Asian proverb

Life is partly what we make it,
and partly what is made
by the friends we choose.

Señor Coyote

A PLAY

from a Mexican legend

Characters

Narrator

Señor Rabbit

Señor Snake

Señor Coyote

Narrator   Once upon a time
a big rock fell on Señor Snake.

Señor Snake   Help! Help!

Señor Rabbit   Maybe Señor Snake
is trying to trick me. But
maybe he really needs help.

Narrator   Señor Rabbit was afraid
of Señor Snake. But he still
wanted to help.

54

Señor Rabbit   Maybe I can push
the rock off your back.

Señor Snake   Push it off, and
I will give you a reward.

Narrator   Señor Rabbit pushed
and pushed. At last he pushed
the rock off Señor Snake.

55

Señor Snake   Can you guess
what your reward will be?

Señor Rabbit   No. What?

Señor Snake   I am going to eat
you up. That is
your reward.

Señor Rabbit　That is not fair.
I helped you.　I pushed the rock
off your back.

Señor Snake　I needed help then.
But now I do not need help.
So I will eat you up.

Señor Rabbit　No!　That is not fair!

Señor Snake　Yes!　That is fair!

Narrator   They asked Señor Coyote
to decide what was fair.

Señor Coyote   I need to see
how things were. Let me push
the rock back on you, Señor Snake.

Señor Snake   Very well.
  Take a good look, Señor Coyote.
  Now get this rock off me.

Señor Coyote   Now I see.
  Señor Snake, it is fair
  for you to have the rock
  as your reward.

59

Caterpillar
by
CHRISTINA ROSSETTI

Brown and furry
Caterpillar in a hurry,
Take your walk
To the shady leaf or stalk.
Spin and die,
To live again a butterfly.

Where I Can Dance

an African folktale

There once was a man
who saw a well in the desert.

He looked in the well.
He saw no water.
But he saw a goat!

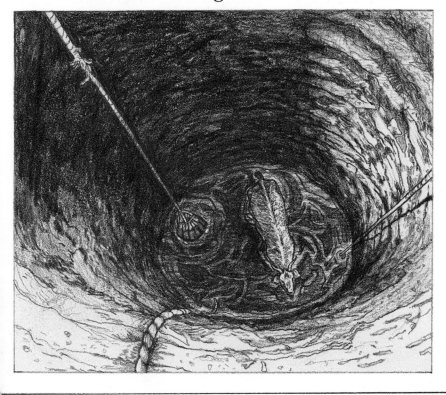

A goat had fallen
into the well.

The man saw a trader
coming with two camels.
"Maybe I can play
a trick on this trader,"
he said.

When the trader was nearby,
the man pulled out the goat.

"What is this?" said the trader.

"This is my goat well," he said.
"I pull out a new goat each day."

"I'll trade you my camels
for your goat well," said the trader.
"Take them. But before you go,
tell me your name."

The man said, "My name is
Where-I-Can-Dance."
And away he went.

The next day, the trader
looked in the well.
No goat.

All day he stayed at the well.
Still no goat.
Then he knew
he had been tricked.

So he went after the man
named Where-I-Can-Dance.

The trader came to a village.

He asked a girl, "Do you know
Where-I-Can-Dance?"

"You can dance here," she said.

"No, no," he said.
"I am asking if you know
Where-I-Can-Dance."

Again the girl said,
"You can dance here."

67

He shook his head. "Take me
to the Wise Woman of the village.
Maybe she will know
Where-I-Can-Dance."

The Wise Woman smiled.
"You were tricked," she said.
"Tricked with a goat well.
And tricked with a name."

She told the girl, "A new man
with two camels is in our village.
Tell him that someone named
What-I-Must-Do wants him."

The man came at once.

He asked, "Do you know
What-I-Must-Do?"

"Yes, I know what you must do,"
she said. "Give back the camels."

Then he saw the trader.
He knew he had been tricked
with the very trick he played.

"Oh, Wise Woman," he said.
"You tricked me well.
I will give back the camels
and go back to my goat well."

71

"Goat well?" said the girl
in surprise. "I will go with you.
Never have I seen a goat well."

"And you never will,"
said the Wise Woman.
And she shook her head.

UNIT THREE
The Whole
Story

Three Billy Goats Gruff

a Norwegian fairy tale

Once upon a time
there were three goats—
Little Billy Goat Gruff,
Middle Billy Goat Gruff,
and Big Billy Goat Gruff.

They wanted to cross the bridge
and climb up the hill to eat.

But a wicked troll
lived under the bridge.

Little Billy Goat Gruff
started to cross the bridge.
Trip-trap. Trip-trap.

The wicked troll roared,
"Who is trip-trapping
over my bridge?"

"Little Billy Goat Gruff,"
said the goat.

"I'm going to
gobble you up,"
roared the troll.

78

"No! Not me. I'm so little,"
cried Little Billy Goat Gruff.
"Wait for Middle Billy Goat Gruff."

"Oh, very well. Go!"
roared the troll.

So Little Billy Goat Gruff
crossed the bridge and
climbed up the hill to eat.

Soon Middle Billy Goat Gruff
started to cross the bridge.
Trip-trap. Trip-trap.

The wicked troll roared,
"Who is trip-trapping
over my bridge?"

"Middle Billy Goat Gruff,"
said the goat.

"I'm going to gobble you up,"
roared the troll.

"No! No! I'm not very big,"
cried Middle Billy Goat Gruff.
"Wait for Big Billy Goat Gruff."

"Oh, very well. Go!"
roared the troll.

So Middle Billy Goat Gruff
crossed the bridge and
climbed up the hill to eat.

Soon Big Billy Goat Gruff
started to cross the bridge.
Trip-trap. Trip-trap.

The wicked troll roared,
"Who is trip-trapping
over my bridge?"

"Big Billy Goat Gruff,"
said the goat.

"I'm going to
gobble you up,"
roared the troll.

"Oh, no! No, you're not!"
said Big Billy Goat Gruff.

The wicked troll roared.
He climbed up on the bridge.

Big Billy Goat Gruff rushed
at him—POW!
He knocked the troll
off the bridge.

And that was the end
of the wicked troll.

From then on,
the three Billy Goats Gruff
crossed the bridge every day
and climbed up the hill to eat.

UNIT FOUR

Numbers,
Nature, and
Nonsense

One, Two, Three, Four, Five
from
MOTHER GOOSE

One, two, three, four, five.
Once I caught a fish alive.

Six, seven, eight, nine, ten.
Then I let it go again.

Why did you let it go?
Because it bit my finger so.

Which finger did it bite?
The little finger on the right.

The Ugly Duckling

by

HANS CHRISTIAN ANDERSEN

There were many sunny spots by the river. In the sunniest spot stood an old mansion.

Mrs. Duck sat nearby on her eggs. "I wish they'd hatch," she said to an old duck.

IN THE SUNNIEST SPOT STOOD AN OLD MANSION

Just then, one egg cracked.
Out came a little duckling.

The old duck said,
"The biggest egg has not cracked.
Maybe it's a turkey egg."

At last, it cracked!
And out came the biggest chick.

94

"He is ugly," said Mrs. Duck.

"Maybe he is a turkey."

Mrs. Duck took her ducklings down to the river.

They jumped in after her, one by one.

Mrs. Duck looked at the big ugly duckling. "That is no turkey," she said. "Look how he swims."

She took her ducklings
back to the mansion.
The big ducks pointed
at the ugly duckling
and laughed.
One of them flew at him.

The poor ugly duckling
ran to the barn.

A hen said to him,
"My, but you are ugly!
What kind of bird are you?"

A cat chased him outside.
He ran to the river
and swam away.

He swam and swam.
Away from the ducks.
Away from the mansion.
Away from all the turkeys and
swans and hens that lived there.

That night the ugly duckling
crept into an old woman's house.

"What is this?" said the woman.
"It looks a little like a duck.
But what an ugly one!"

The woman's hen went up to him.
"Can you lay eggs?" she asked.
"No," he said.
"Then out you go!" said the hen.

Soon the days grew colder.
When the ugly duckling crept
indoors, children chased him away.

But sunny days came back at last.
He swam up to the old mansion
where he was hatched.

There he saw three swans.
"They will chase me away," he said.

Then he looked at himself
in the water.

He was big now and beautiful!
No longer was he an ugly duckling!
Now he was a swan.

A boy from the mansion pointed
at him. "Look at the new one.
The new one's the prettiest."

The ugly duckling was now
the prettiest swan.

Autumn Fires

by

ROBERT LOUIS STEVENSON

Sing a song of seasons,
Something bright in all,
Flowers in the summer,
Fires in the fall.

April Showers

from

MOTHER GOOSE

April showers
bring May flowers.

The Magic Pot
a tall tale

There was once a girl
who lived with her mother.
An old woman gave this girl
a magic pot.

She said to the girl,
"Say, 'Cook, little pot, cook.'
And it will cook porridge.
Say, 'Stop, little pot, stop.'
And it will stop cooking."

When her mother came in, the girl said, "Cook, little pot, cook."

It filled up with porridge. And they ate all they wanted.

Then she said, "Stop, little pot, stop." And it stopped.

One day the girl went out.
Her mother said, "Cook,
little pot, cook."
It filled up
with porridge.

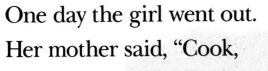

She ate all she wanted.
Then she said, "No more, little pot."
But the pot cooked and cooked.
Soon porridge was all over the table.

111

The mother cried, "Little pot, don't cook so much."

But the pot cooked and cooked. Soon porridge was all over the table and all over the floor.

The mother tried to think
of the words the girl said.
But she could not.
"NO MORE!" she cried.
But that did not make
the pot stop.

Then the girl came back.
She saw porridge
all over the table,
all over the floor,
and running out the door.

She did not want to step
in it. But she had to.

Her mother cried,
"I said to the pot, 'No more!'
But it did not stop."

The girl said, "Stop, little pot, stop." And the pot stopped.

But for days, she and her mother were stepping in porridge.

Yankee Doodle

from
MOTHER GOOSE

Yankee Doodle came to town,
Riding on a pony.
He stuck a feather in his cap
And called it macaroni.

117

A·C·K·N·O·W·L·E·D·G·M·E·N·T·S

Acknowledgment is gratefully made to the following publisher for permission to reprint this selection.

"Snail." From *Selected Poems* by Langston Hughes. © 1947 by Langston Hughes. Reprinted by permission of Alfred A. Knopf, Inc.

The following poems are excerpted from longer poems in consideration of the ages of the readers:

"Snail" by Langston Hughes

"Caterpillar" by Christina Rossetti

"Autumn Fires" by Robert Louis Stevenson

I·L·L·U·S·T·R·A·T·I·O·N C·R·E·D·I·T·S

Acknowledgment is gratefully made to the following individuals and publishers for permission to reprint these illustrations.

PAGE	ILLUSTRATOR
8	Blanche Fisher Wright. From *The Real Mother Goose.* © 1916 by Checkerboard Press, Inc. Used with permission.
9	Jessie Willcox Smith.
10	C. L. Fraser.
11	Henriette Willebeek le Mair. © 1994 by Soefi Stichting Inayat Fundatie Sirdar. Reprinted by permission of East-West Publications (U.K.) Ltd.
12, 21	Wanda Gág. Reprinted by permission of Coward-McCann, Inc. from "The Musicians of Bremen" from *Tales from Grimm,* © 1936 by Wanda Gág. © renewed 1964 by Robert Janssen.
13–15, 18	Frederick Richardson. From *Great Children's Stories.* © 1923 by Checkerboard Press, Inc. Used with permission.
17	Arthur Rackham.
20	Pamela R. Levy. © 1994 by Jamestown Publishers, Inc. All rights reserved.
22–23	Katharine Sturges.
24	Fern Bisel Peat. Courtesy of Blue Lantern Studio, Seattle, Washington.
26–39	Randolph Caldecott. From *Our Caldecott's Picture Book,* courtesy of the Providence Athenaeum.
40	Dorothy M. Wheeler. Courtesy of Blue Lantern Studio, Seattle, Washington.
41	J. E. Rogers.
43	Milo Winter. From *The Aesop for Children* illustrated by Milo Winter. © 1919 by Checkerboard Press, Inc. Used with permission.
46–50	Maryjane Begin. © 1994 by Maryjane Begin.

120